The Scarecrow Competition

Jack's farm was entering a scarecrow competition, and Jack's parents gave him the important task of making their scarecrows look special. But how many scarecrows are there? Lets count them together in French!

Un, deux, trois, quatre. There are four.

The languasaurus had an idea. He'd seen in the shed an old bag full of clothes. They could dress the scarecrows in these!

"What was **une robe**?" thought Jack. He had no idea!

Une robe was a dress!

So they dressed one of the scarecrows in **une robe**.

"une robe"

They also found in the bag a hat with a matching ribbon and flower.

Jack thought it looked fantastic.

The languasaurus then pulled something else out of the bag and said "**Un t-shirt**."

"Is that a t-shirt? " asked Jack.

Un t-shirt was indeed a t-shirt.

But there were a few **t-shirts** in the bag. Lets count how many there were:

They put the t-shirts on the three other scarecrows:

Jack thought the scarecrows looked fantastic. But they needed to make the scarecrows look even better! So Jack asked the languasaurus what else was in the bag.

"**Un jean**" said the Languasaurus.

"Hmm. That sounds like jeans" thought Jack. But is he right?

Yes! Jack was right! **Un jean** was indeed jeans!

So they dressed one of the scarecrows in **un jean**.

The languasaurus then pulled something else out of the bag and said "**Une jupe**." Jack had no idea what this could be….

Une jupe was a skirt. Hmm. Interesting. He didn't know that. So they dressed one of the scarecrows in **une jupe**.

The languasaurus then pulled one final thing out of the bag and said "**Un short**." "Is that shorts?" asked Jack.

Un short was indeed shorts.
They dressed the final scarecrow in **un short**.
Jack thought it all looked fantastic. And it did!

During the night Jack was worried as he could hear strong winds whirling around outside. The following day Jack and the languasaurus went to see how the scarecrows were.

The scarecrows were ruined! Jack was so upset he ran inside!

The languasaurus worked hard all day and all night restoring the scarecrows. The following day Jack couldn't believe his eyes when he saw the scarecrows in the field. Let's count in French how many scarecrows there were: Un, deux, trois, quatre, cinq.

"They are all here!" shouted Jack. He then said "m**erci**" as that's how the French say thank you. But then Jack noticed there was an extra one! And the extra one didn't look like the other scarecrows!

The languasaurus explained that **un nounours** was a teddy bear, and that they could have a teddy bear's picnic as a theme. Hmm. adding u**n nounours** was a good idea!

They then checked they had all the clothes they needed. Let's say them in French with Jack:

 **une robe**

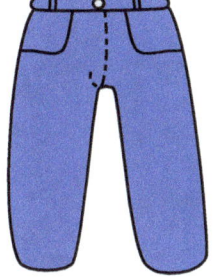 **un jean**

 **une jupe**

 **un short**

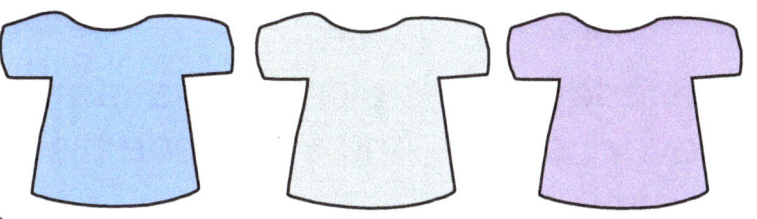 **trois t-shirts**

Jack came forth in the competition, so there was no prize. But he was not sad because it had been s*o much* fun to do. Besides, the scarecrows looked fantastic. They had even added some toy food. They were something to be proud of.

People came from afar to see the teddy bear's picnic. The farm shop and café were busier than ever before! And this made his parents very happy and proud of him.

The Treasure Hunt

One cloudy morning when Jack went to see the languasaurus he didn't look his usual cheerful self, so the languasaurus asked him how he was.

Jack said he was only feeling so so as he had a bit of a headache.

"Maybe some fresh air would help to get rid of the headache" thought the languasaurus. So he told Jack he thought there could be treasure hidden somewhere on the farm!

Jack liked the idea of a treasure hunt, so the languasaurus handed him a note. On it there was just two words…..

Jack asked if **le café** was the café, and the languasaurus replied o**ui,** as that's how the French say yes.

So they ran to **le café**.

The looked all over the place at **le café**. Where was the next clue? Suddenly Jack found it. Again on the piece of paper were just two words……

Jack asked if **les toilettes** were the toilets, and the languasaurus replied **oui**, as that's how the French say yes.

So they ran to **les toilettes**.

This time it was the languasaurus who found the next clue.

On the piece of paper there were just two words…

Jack had to think about this one for a moment. What did it sound the most like? He eventually asked if **le lac** was the lake.

It was! So they ran quickly to **le lac**. Jack wanted to be first there!

Jack soon spotted on the fence the next clue. But what did it say?

Jack read aloud the clue: "**le magasin**." But he had no idea what it meant. Would he ever find the treasure if he didn't understand the clue? Luckily for Jack, his friend was able to tell him that **le magasin** was the shop. So they quickly ran to **le magasin**.

It didn't take long for Jack and the languasaurus to find the next clue. But where was the treasure? Would they ever find it?

On the next clue it said…..

Jack asked if **le parking** was the car park, and the languasaurus said yes in French.

They were getting tired, so they just walked to **le parking**!

Where was the next clue? Or would they find the treasure?

Let's say in French all the places on the farm where Jack had been looking for the treasure:

But where was the next clue or the treasure?

Something suddenly caught Jack's eye in the corner of the car park.

It was **le trésor**! The treasure!

It was actually Jack's toy money that he had put a long time ago in the shed! But Jack said nothing of this to the languasaurus.

It had been such a fun treasure hunt, and a special day that he would never forget. And his headache, well, that cleared up ages ago!

© Joanne Leyland   First edition 2018   Second edition 2021
The useful words and phrases and the song lyrics that follow may be photocopied by the purchasing individual or institution for class or home use. The rest of the book may not be photocopied or reproduced electronically without the prior agreement of the author.

Useful French words and phrases

C'est fantastique! - - - - - It's fantastic
Oui - - - - - - - - - - - - - - - - - Yes

Comment ça va? - - - - - How are you?
Comme ci comme ça - - So so

1 – un
2 – deux
3 – trois
4 – quatre
5 – cinq

une robe
(a dress)

un t-shirt
(a t-shirt)

un nounours
(a teddybear)

un jean
(jeans)

un short
(shorts)

une jupe
(a skirt)

le café
(the cafe)

les toilettes
(the toilets)

le lac
(the lake)

le magasin
(the shop)

le parking
(the car park)

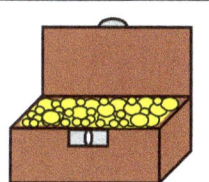
le trésor
(the treasure)

© Joanne Leyland - This page may be photocopied by the purchasing individual or institution for use in class or at home

Let's sing a song!

The following words could either be sung to a made up tune, or you could try saying the words as a rap.

For inspiration of a melody to use you could hum first a nursery rhyme. How many different versions can you create using the lyrics?

il y a, il y a

 le café, le café

 les toilettes, les toilettes

 le lac, le lac

il y a, il y a

 le magasin, le magasin

 le parking, le parking

 le trésor, le trésor

il y a = there is / there are

Follow on activity: Take 5 small pieces of paper, and on each write one of the following:
    le café   les toilettes   le lac   le magasin   le parking
Then turn over this page and see if you can arrange the places in the order they appear in the story "The treasure hunt". Check back in the story to see if you are right!

© Joanne Leyland - This page may be photocopied by the purchasing individual or institution for use in class or at home

www.ingramcontent.com/pod-product-compliance
Lightning Source LLC
Chambersburg PA
CBHW081400080526
44588CB00016B/2553